Books by Corey Mesler:

For Toby, Everything for Toby
Ten Poets
Piecework
Chin-Chin in Eden
Dark on Purpose
The Hole in Sleep
The Agoraphobe's Pandiculations
The Lita Conversation
The Chloe Poems
Some Identity Problems
Pictures from Lang and Fellini
Grit
The Tense Past
Talk: A Novel in Dialogue
We Are Billion-Year-Old Carbon
Short Story and Other Short Stories
Following Richard Brautigan
Publisher
Listen: 29 Short Conversations
The Ballad of the Two Tom Mores
The Narcoleptic Therapist and Other Stories
Notes Toward the Story and Other Stories

Before the Great Troubling

Poems by Corey Mesler

ISBN 978-1-936373-15-4

© 2011 Corey Mesler. All rights reserved. No part of this publication may be reproduced or transmitted in any form or by any means, electronic or mechanical, without permission in writing from the publisher. Requests for permission to make copies of any part of this work should be e-mailed to info@unboundcontent.com.
Published in the United States by Unbound Content, LLC, Englewood, NJ.
Cover art: Hiding in Shadow © 2011, by Rebecca Tickle.
The poems in this collection are all original and previously unpublished with the exception of those listed in the credits page at the end of the volume.

Before the Great Troubling
First edition 2011

For Cheryl, and in memory of Max and Dot Hodges. With special thanks to Rebecca Tickle for editorial assistance.

Table of Contents

Opening 11
Opening 2 12
Regret 13
Memoir 14
The Poem of the World 15
Out Again 16
Pull My Daisy 17
Removing Stumps 18
Simply Again Simply 20
Summer Fanstast 21
We Were Told to Wait Here 22
The Barbarian Heart 23
Ash 24
13 Ways of Looking at a Blackboard 25
Life During Wartime 26
Pray 27
The Observer Observed 28
The Halloween Between Us 29
The Fairy Tale Wife 30
Bell's Palsy 1 31
Educationalist 32
My Thomas Pynchon 33
Sandra, I Am Almost Finished 34
Joe Zen 35
Elvis in Elvisland 36
Chloe at Three 38
Flower Girl 39
First There Is a Mountain 40
Colloquy in the Void 41
After Reading *The Tao of the Jump Shot* 42
An Email Poem 43

The Comma	44
Nature Jar	45
The Infection of City	46
Tell Me if You Think This Is Gonna Be a Problem	47
A Treasure Hid in a Field	48
We Are All Connected	49
In the Salinger Building There Are Nine Stories	50
See Me	51
The Sleeping Saviors	52
Those Hitchcock Silences	54
Those Melville Silences	55
My Father's Death Is a Small Box	56
Sleepe, Angry Beauty	57
Nightstand Poem	58
Our History of the Book	59
In My Dream Emily Mortimer	60
The First Lovefall	61
My Novel Life	62
My Dog Talks to Me	64
Hell, the Whole Kingdom Sucks	65
My John Lennon Period	66
The Monkey and the Mountain	67
First You Walk	68
Someone Told Me It's All Happening at the Zoo	69
Jack and the Tower of Babel	70
Bookseller	71
Sortilege	72
Hoagy Carmichael's Cigarette	73
It Was a Test Was What They Told Us	74
Remember My Name	75
Poem Written at Night in September of 2001	76
The Thomas Pynchon Tower	77
Nocturne	78

My Aunt Agni	79
Backspace	80
An Afternoon at the Ono Lennons	81
Cloudmountaincalling	82
There's a Long Line at the New Poem	83
The Instructions: How to Get There	84
The Box	85
It Was That Kind of Hero, Sweetheart	86
Phoenix	87
Our First Voyage to Ataraxia	88
The Committee in My Head	90
How the Hero One Day Sat	91
The Man With the Perfect Jump Shot	92
God	94
Recent Developments in Home Schooling	95
Closer to Home	96
KKK	97
The Judge's Narcolepsy	98
Lizard	99
Watching Things Fall From a Distance	100
Corinthian	101
Knitting	102
Execution	103
Voice	104
Too Much Talk	105
Passing a Playground at Night	106
Habitant	107
Chloe at Dusk	108
Graceland	109
A Penultimate Parley	110
Before the Great Troubling	111
About the Author	112
List of Publication Credits	113

Somewhere inside something there is a rush of greatness ...
—Ragni, Rado, McDermott, from *Hair*

Only a mountain knows the inside of another mountain.
—Frida Kahlo

Opening

The door is opening.
A child emerges.
It's our child.
We vow to begin the
day as if it were
our best engine.
The child's eyes are
full of life.
We believe it is our
life. The door
stands open.
The light coming through
is soft as gathered wool.
Our hold on the day
is precarious.
We gather briefly to
pray, to say the
old words again.
The world briefly cracks
open, an egg.

Opening 2

I stand in the simplest line.
The movement is only
here, between the eyes.
The words drop like rain.
The world conforms or doesn't.
The children sing the newest
songs. They go through.
I wait for the rain to wet me,
or stop. I wait, careworn.
I stand in the simplest line.

Regret

In the waning light
I type the words
"waning light."
I'm not the poet I mean
to be, nor
am I a man
who takes advantage of
that last
bit of light.

Memoir

I wrote the story of my life with
a burning stick. I lied
on every page. When it came time
to leave the cave I said
to my wife, a comely simian, I
want to tell everyone my
story. I want them to listen to me
just as goddamn hard as
we wait for the God to whom we
pray. She smiled her softest
pity. She loves me without question.
She loves the lie I live, the
lie that will take me away from her,
if only for fame, or for money.

The Poem of the World

The poem makes the world.
This is the job of the poem.
In the morning there is fresh
ink. In the evening there is
a last thought, a fidget, before sleep.
And then the irresistible dream.

Out Again

We were afraid of
the sky.
This was the pen-
ultimate shame.
We held hands
with the children,
wishing for them
a different way.
We were outside a
lot at this time.
We tried
watching our shoes
as we made
our way down every side-
walk. We
fell before we could say
to the children,
watch your step, too.
Each night,
before the prayer
about not waking,
we named the ways in
which the world,
the old mechanical world,
still worked.
We called out the names
of the strong
like a litany of temporary
penates. We said,
save us from ourselves.
Invite us indoors.
Save us,
we are God's children,
surely not the last of the potty.

Pull My Daisy

Jack Kerouac and Allen Ginsberg
made love on a small bed
in a crappy apartment in San
Francisco. Afterwards Jack drew
a daisy on Allen's midsection
and Allen wrote a poem about Jack'
s Johnny. Jack quickly took
to drink and Allen worked long into
the night, breathing into
the fetid air words that hung there like
stars against the Bible black.

Removing Stumps

My father, broad-backed
and sweating, would dig
a moat around the thing,
chopping at exposed roots
with a long-handled ax.
He let me take a few swings.
"Your uncle split his foot
with one of these," he told
me, as I hacked like a thin-
limbed girl. Some of them
he drilled holes in, filled
the holes with motor oil
and let them burn slowly.
Taking out stumps was an
all-day adventure. By the
time I left home our lot
had been reduced from 72
trees to a sturdy half-dozen.
The wilderness we moved
into in 1961 became a suburb
overnight. I saw my father,
not as a developer or despoiler
of the natural landscape, but
as a man, larger than life,
whose hands were like vises,
whose arms were thick with
veins. I am not that kind of
man. Here in middle-age
I reflect on this and know
that I am *other*, defeated by
tools, letting trees have their
tangled, hard-won territory.

I could no more remove a stump
than fly. Instead I show my
son the latest poem I've had
published, hoping he sees in it
something magical, something
only a superman could manage.

Simply Again Simply

I will try to tell you the simple thing.
I will not reach for the thesaurus (a
reference book of words that
mean the same thing). I will slide the
note under your door while
you are away. When you find it its
simplicity will appeal to you
in simple ways. I will pretend that
this is how love starts, and poetry
(the art of rhythmical composition).

Summer Fantast

A woman made of cake,
a desirable woman.
A picture worth a thousand
worries, a sexy picture.
The day so hot it makes us
stupid. The night still
hot, full of secret sounds,
full of the stuff dreams are
made from. The dreams
full of mystery, desire, and
the coiling embrace of
a woman, a woman made of cake.

We Were Told to Wait Here

In the end…everything will be found to be true of everybody.
—Lawrence Durrell

It's midnight at the end of the
universe and the temperature
needs adjusting. The dogs
are all spayed. They look at us
with the eyes of the crucified,
the ones *next to* Christ.
All the calls are from our friends
at the bank. They want their
money back. We wear sunglasses
because we don't want to see
the sun. The one next to the thieves.
It's midnight at the end of a
long trip back to where we started.
The friends we had are friends, still.
They pierce us with little pins.
They line up to hear what we say to
the bank. We say, arf. We say, oof.
It's what the dogs taught us,
right before, you know, we crucified
them. It's midnight. It's the end
of something we never wanted to
start. We answer the phone with
a blowtorch. The callers shimmer
in the heat. They shine like Christ.

The Barbarian Heart

For the haiku poets, the cry of a mosquito is just as important as a general's hat or a storm.
—Robert Bly

Basho and I sat in the moonlight.
In his lap he held a trout.
Basho signaled to me that
the trout was about to speak.
I discovered that my pen was a stone.
The moonlight began to sing.

Ash

Like a fire
I want

to once again

drink
the dew

from
the flower

betweenyourlegs.

13 Ways of Looking at a Blackboard

1. Stare at the background until the words disappear.
2. Stare at the words, ingesting them, until the blackboard could be any dreamspace.
3. Through one eye only, fist over the other, sleep calling.
4. Through the eyes of Wendy Ceccerelli, who sits beside you and whose pigtails make you fancy a world made of light and chimera.
5. Through one eye only, half your face palsied, perhaps only temporarily.
6. Stand up and shout, Viva la revolucion! Down with the books of the oppressors!
7. Through x-ray specs, after noting the new substitute wears panties as thin as the lap of water.
8. While holding the hand of your best friend, Pat, arrested for smoking and writing the words to "Subterranean Homesick Blues" on the stall wall.
9. While holding the hand of Wendy Ceccerelli (see above), sweating.
10. With one shoe off, inside of which rests, like a yolk in an egg, the test answers.
11. Naked, unprepared for the test, the final exam.
12. Sleeping, dreaming of being naked, unprepared for the test, the final exam.
13. Holding the hand of Laura Anderson, the ugliest girl in the class, who has a crush on you which you are well aware of, which you ignore, which you pray the bigger boys will not discover until school is over and Laura Anderson is transformed from toad to princess, and you from boy to man, from boy to man.

Life During Wartime

In Louis Malle's *Black Moon*
the unicorn is fat and dull.
The naked children scrabbling
after the pig represent
something or other.
The young girl, wandering the
wartorn landscape,
is lovely like a rill.
Eventually, she finds Family
but the fairy tale
threatens to engulf her. And the
pet rat has a name.
We should all live like this in
wartime. We should all
look to the Archetype for adjustment,
for the way out of the
dream. We should all understand that
the way out is the way further in.

Pray

Say it. The poem lies doggo.
The lies are black, marks
in sand. The dog makes
new sounds, wanting only to
be let out. Say it. The last
word will be had by Poem.
Say it. The last god is Word.

The Observer Observed

It's just a picture, a
woman in a red dress.
I drink it in
as if it were a phthisis.
I imagine I am always
looking to be stirred
because I am
so often shaken.
I write her name on
an asterisk. I
stand in the rain all
day waiting for answers.
The picture keeps mum.
Its secret is that
I am also important.

The Halloween Between Us

We set the pumpkin on the porch
as if it were our child in a basket.
The night was torn, dark slashes
across the sheets. The moon appeared.
You reached for my heart laid
suddenly open. I tried to make up the
difference in your eyes, just as
the wolfman came in in the wolfman's disguise.

The Fairy Tale Wife

It's dark in the kitchen.
It's where they've chained her.
Her smile is like that
first apple, the one without the
poison. He approaches her
from the rear. It's how
he enters the fairy tale. He takes
her because that's how
it was written once upon a time.
She turns afterwards
toward him, her destination.
Her heart is sore. He
is like a wind, a beastly breeze.
He returns night after
night. He brings her stories
from other homes.
He brings her a bouquet of forks.

Bell's Palsy 1

Face half dead, a metaphor
I need like a hole in the
ozone. How strange it feels.
How swift it came.
Like lightning on a clear day:
suddenly I am dribbling
asparagus juice into my beard.
Suddenly I am only
half-blinking. The other eye,
the one that is suddenly
not-me, blurs, stays open
stubbornly, dries and knows
little. It is the eye, though,
that sees where this poem
is going, sad little poem,
unsure how alive even it is.
It's a poem that wants to grasp
the ineffable. Do you know
such poems? Like speaking
from the side of my mouth,
like writing and only half-meaning
it. Only you will listen to me
now. Only you with your
open heart. Stay beside me so
I can whisper to you the half-truths
I am seeking, here with half
a facade, my love, half-heartedly.

Educationalist

I went to the mountain
because I had tired
of telling the old story
to friends and not-friends.
The mountain did not
greet me. Nor did it even turn
when I approached.
I practice now every day.
The shade of the mountain
comes and goes.
I try to reason that it is right
for it to come and go.
The mountain taunts my reason.

My Thomas Pynchon

I left my Thomas Pynchon in the rain.
It's swollen now to proportions
even Mr. P could not have envisaged.
And new characters have emerged,
a one-armed pitcher, a man whose
heart is literally on his sleeve,
a python with a paintbox.
I look at the new Pynchon with a
reverence I normally reserve for
those TV shows depicting the
afterlife. I settle into my settee now
and the children lift the Pynchon for
me. Their little arms shake like shadows
holding it up. Their expressions,
so rapt, so severe, say, Daddy
loves his fiction, he loves his fiction.

Sandra, I Am Almost Finished

Sandra, I am almost finished
writing about you. Your death
stands next to my desk,
its skeletal hand on my shoulder.
With every word I shake a
little harder. After your name I
am afraid of the period. I am
afraid to be almost finished with you.

Joe Zen

The best coffee
of the day
is the sip
taken from the cold cup
on the counter
leftover
from the morning
when you made it fresh,
wife and
daughter still sleeping.

Elvis in Elvisland

The cacophony of voices that have joined together to create a chorus of informed opinion, uninformed speculation, hagiography, symbolism, and blame, can be difficult to drown out, but in the end there is only one voice that counts.
—Peter Guralnick

Let's imagine this:
He's on the set of *Clambake*
or *Stay Away, Joe.*
He's lip-synching something
insipid about uh huh
there goes my dream girl.
He's barely hitting the marks,
barely feigning singing,
barely there. He's running
on hematic speed. Let's imagine
it strikes him that he's
just sausage now, that he's
lost something, given
it away, or had it stolen,
his life-force, his soul.
Now, let's say, that he doesn't
give a shit because he's
part of a money machine,
a vital part. The enabler.
It's a believable parable.

But, it's not true. We know
it's not. He felt himself
die a little bit on
every cheesy set, a little
bit during every perfunctory
song: The man who invented
something startling,
a long time ago, in a little
alchemical shop called Sun,
in a mystical time called
The Fifties, in a corrupt and enchanted
fiefdom called America.

Chloe at Three

Little fingers
slick with jam

I take them into my
bear-sized paw

and wonder at
how something so

delicate can tear such
a large hole in me.

Flower Girl

She picks a bell-shaped flower
and puts it in a small medicine
bottle to give to her ailing
teacher. Chloe, at six, already
a nurturer, loves the growing,
glowing things of this world.
Just down the street a sunflower
stands twice her height.
She strains toward its face, and
one can't help but think,
it quietly strains back toward hers.

First There Is a Mountain, Then There Is No Mountain, Then There Is

It was a field, a field of study.
She was a lass, a problem in geometry.
We lay there in the grass
counting our stars. She took off her
cabinet and I opened like yesterday's mail.
She said, I want to be nothing
to you. I said, yes, there are currents
underwater as beautiful as any wave.
She looked toward the horizon.
There was a straight line there, drawn by
some celestial monkey.
I asked her if there was a future and
she pointed toward the hills, now swelling
with apposition. I looked toward
the horizon, too, a straight line, drawn by
water, drawn by the unbuckling
of the Earth's dirty trousers.
She said, it is not our way to speak in
riddles. I said, I know a way
to the mountain that doesn't involve the
path, now spackled with starlight.
She only squinted harder and said her
eyesight was going, going
into the hills, now suddenly smaller, like our
ambitions, like our goddamned
affair never to be spoken of again, our love.

Colloquy in the Void

He said, it's quiet here without God.
I said, isn't it cold, the way
your hand touches nothing.
He said, I used to know a man who
could talk his way into sleepwalking.
He said, I used to know ways
to get women to stroke me.
I said, isn't it quiet here without hands.
He said, God, I used to know you.
I said, don't talk anymore. He said, yes,
let's be quiet. Let's watch it all end.

After Reading *The Tao of the Jump Shot*

The arc of the ball in flight
is half the circle of truth.
The sound it makes passing
through the hoop is the sound
of cranes lifting from a pond.
The arm still extended shall
stay extended. The body
released shall stay released.

An Email Poem

An email poem
must be short,
the attention span of the
internet fan
like a butterfly.
And like a butterfly
the email poem
has broken its first home
and now unfolds
its multicolored wings
and virtually
disappears behind you,
into the drunkards'
chat room.

The Comma

The comma is key, a small
key. It says, wait a second.
This is the same command
I occasionally have to give
the devil, as he takes my breath
away. This is the same sug-
gestion I give to you, my lover,
the woman who waits with
me. The comma is a small key.
It turns right here, in my heart,
where the sentence is carried out.

Nature Jar

The snail shell my daughter finds
on the sidewalk is dried out,
a mossy something in its whorl.
She loves it anyway and puts it
in her nature jar, next to the locust
husk, the exanimate moth, the
firefly she thought would burn forever.

The Infection of City

It is a naked city. Faith is not pampered, nor hope encouraged; there is no place to lay one's exhaustion: but instead pinnacles skewer it undisguised against vacancy.
—William Gaddis

I wait all night for the light
to change to green. It's
never spring in Heartache City.
The man to the left of me
thinks he's right. It's hard to say
because it's hard to see. The
ice storm has lasted a fortnight.
In the fort, nights, the soldiers are
sandbagging the TV. Their dolls
have all been confiscated. I wait
all night for the right light.
It's all I have left. I used to speak
your name to the animals.
Now I'm lucky if their tales
don't hurt. Look up ahead, the
seer tells me. I can't raise mine
or I would heed. He'd just as soon
be shed of me. I appreciate his
lack of tenderness. It's all I left.
Tomorrow and tomorrow in
Heartache City is where I'll be.
Look me up even if down. I
will almost love you, my Vacancy.

Tell Me if You Think This Is Gonna Be a Problem

The doctor poked me with a stick.
I turned on the spit
until my face showed the burn.
They gathered round
in their cowls and gowns, seemingly
dispassionate and smart.
Yet I stumped them, this quivering
meat, these popping petards.
Another doctor went for a sharper stick.
They all nodded. Now, we'll
see, they mustered. I lay there, an ex-
posed nerve, an ex-propositis.
The room seemed a carnival to me,
spinning colors and dis-
torted music, clowns and noise, and
there in the middle of it
my role: freak. Even to the experts,
my saviors, the rapists.

A Treasure Hid in a Field

The lock on the keyboard
didn't work. I spoke
to the assembly about the
menace of assembly.
In the paper I find my name
with a letter beside it.
It's a Greek letter. I don't
understand, nor do I
have time for such fribble.
I write this down with
a burnt stick. What
stays is the attitude, the constant
consonant. Really, I
say to my family, don't come
to me for homework
anymore. I'm a desiccated husk,
a wastrel. As I leave I
say one last thing, not expecting
it to last. Everyone turns
a deaf ear. This is as it should
be, here in the gibbet
shadow, the last show on Earth.

We Are All Connected

I wrote a single word
on a fallen leaf

and gave it to my daughter.
Her tiny hand held

it for a moment and then
it was whisked away,

the wind not a fan of
language or its magic.

I looked for that word
for weeks, I'm sorry to say.

Only yesterday I found a
leaf with writing on it;

it seemed like the same
leaf. The word was meaningless,

though, and now I can't remember
if this is our word or not.

Corey Mesler

In the Salinger Building There Are Nine Stories

In the Salinger building
there are nine stories.
Anyone using the street
entrance knows that the
doorman is a gorilla.
There's a place to leave
packages, a long chute.
And up on top, in the sole
room on the ninth floor,
sits a raven, never answering.
Natives show out-of-towners
the Salinger building
and there's always the same
question. What's going
on on the other floors?
Friends, whoever knows isn't
saying. Consider instead
the lobby, replete with pillows,
puzzles and bright crystal mirrors.
It is here that anyone can
find themselves. It is here,
really, that the Salinger
building is the Salinger building.

See Me

On the page blank as a stare
I make a mark.
It is a birthmark. I am born
again here, in
your cold country, in your
deadly, blank eye.
Take me in like a vista. Take
me in like a traveler.
I am not a traveler. I am mote,
only large enough to make you look.

The Sleeping Saviors

The sleeping saviors
in the next room
are filling the house with
snores as sweet
as symphonies.
We tiptoe around, press
our ears to the door,
and listen as if to the
words of skalds.
The sleeping saviors'
dreams are something
else, too. As colorful
as a bush aflame
and as large as the tents
of the gods.
We go there, or imagine
that we do, into
the dreams
of the sleeping saviors.
It is there we are taught
to invent prayers,
personal invocations
that will limn
the infinite and shake the
old Bo-tree
for its glistening fruits.

It all started with the
sleeping saviors,
we say. We say,
we think it is meet and
right that they sleep.
We think it is just what
they needed,
to be free of us for a while.

Those Hitchcock Silences

No one speaks.
The hero is led deeper
into the labyrinth.
He is compelled.
Just as you, deep in your
chair, want to
scream like a void.

Those Melville Silences

after Le Cercle Rouge

Alain Delon smokes the last cigarette
on Earth. He's working on a
caper, of course, and all around him
the French countryside hums
with elegiac tension. Once inside—
where he longs to be—
there is precision and stillness. It's a
zen burglary is what it is.
Afterwards, he bleeds the way we
all will in the end. Even then,
his silence is existential, almost a poem.

My Father's Death Is a Small Box

My father's death is a small box.
In it you will not find his ashes.
Instead look to the stars whose dust
is swept and swept again
over the horizon like the wash of waves.
It's that kind of box. Maybe
you cannot visualize it. Maybe you
never thought that my father's
death could be such a puzzle. I assure
you that it is. And from here it's
still a long way to the stars, and to his death.

Sleepe, Angry Beauty

Let the sleep of the relentless
be mine, the sleep
of forgiving, recompense, sorrow.
My father, dead now 3 years,
my first marriage a
scurvy, my temperament that of
a roiled spado.
I have reached this part partly due
to the implacable love
of one strong woman. Let it be,
let it be just that. Let my
children understand
my last words. Let the sleep that
was my wavering mistress lead
me through the final doors, a sound
hand in mine, one final smile
for all the muck my living stirred.

Nightstand Poem

The one I
didn't
get up and
turn the light on
for
was better
than this.

Our History of the Book

We read the book because it was expected of us.
We were children, really. And the book,
while promising much and delivering little,
became a sort of parent for us. In later days, after
we had forgotten the book and moved on
to building a City, a place of invention and solace,
there were still some of us who would wake
at night with words in our minds, words we wanted
to forget so we could continue our lives in our
sparkling City. We blamed this mental somnambulating
on the book. And when someone brought something
new to the city, a thing with pages and ideas and
that ineffable *something else*, we rightly exiled him.
Often now we make speeches in our city, bright
speeches designed to make us feel better about what
we already have. It is sometimes right that anyone
not listening is exiled also. It's our City after all.
The place we conceived after we put the book behind us.

In My Dream Emily Mortimer

In my dream Emily Mortimer
serves tea, takes my hand
and walks me to the new world.
Everything is blithe and
ruthless and full of fairy light.
In my dream Emily Mortimer
says my name as if it can break
a spell and, in my dream, it
does. I become a man again, shed
the abnormity and rise up ready
to answer all the questions.
The questions have to do with the
dream world and when I wake
they are gone. All that's left is
Emily Mortimer's slim hand in mine,
an enchantment like a hoarfrost.

The First Lovefall

We all went outside.
Love was gathering in puddles
in the declivities of the parish lawn.
It was the first lovefall
and some of us thought we knew how
it would end. Some of
us were optimistic suddenly.
Gayla took me to the basement and
undressed my wounds.
The first lovefall brought this out in
some women. I was happy for it.
It went on loving
till late in the evening. We knew it
was a blessing. We knew
it was the kind of thing we would never
get used to, never take for granted.
Gayla put some love
in the freezer. It was a child's faith
and we adored her for it.
We also knew that love didn't last in
the freezer, but no one had the heart
to tell Gayla this.

My Novel Life

I wrote another novel.
This one I sent
to Singapore
where I heard there was
a sympathetic monk.
I hope to hear back
before I finish
my next novel, the one
about you and me,
the one with all the
estrus. Then I have
another idea, a novel
about the need
to write novels, one
that will approach
the fantastic as if
it is only a traffic cop.
My collected works,
my body of work,
grows up on the
shelf like a fungus.
Nights I write by
its glow, it's that in-
spiring. When I take
a break, if I take a
break, I'll have you over.

We can talk about
all things novel and
anti-novel. It will seem
new to us, nonetheless,
unpracticed as we are
in the ways of
confab. Yet, I love you,
my friend, my best
reader, my sweet audience.
You are everything to
me that my novels are
not. I need you like I
need another plot. I hope
you know how I feel,
when I feel, you know, when
I am between novels.

My Dog Talks to Me

My dog talks to me.
I strive to understand.
She is patient in her lessons.
Yesterday she sat me down
for a half hour discourse.
I nodded and smiled
because humans do that to
show encouragement. I
laughed, I hope, in the right
places. She cocked her
head, sniffed the air, and
went to find a ball to worry.
I sat thinking about what
I had heard, the sense it made.
I was thinking about
the possibility that I will never
be alone again, nor will I
ever again doubt that language
is a prayer within a prayer.

Hell, the Whole Kingdom Sucks

The very first fairy tale princess
waits on the steps of the castle
for the school bus to arrive.
She wears an expression
as tragic as a sponge full of treacle.
It's not the responsibility of being
the very first fairy tale princess.
It's all the teasing on the bus
and in the hallways and
in gym class, her tiara bobbing
as she tries to cry oh so quietly.

My John Lennon Period

I dressed in white. I
listened to the piano as if
it could bring him back.
In his voice I found tears.
In his voice truth.
I woke at all hours to
hear her whispering his name.
I lay on the sidewalk,
my head in a stain,
and let the people step over me.
They were all going
somewhere else. They couldn't
know that I was in
my John Lennon Period.

The Monkey and the Mountain

The monkey went to the mountain
because he had a soft spot
on his soul. The mountain stood for
something willful, something
vainglorious. The monkey made a
small pyre near the base of the
mountain and there he recited his own
shifty sins. The mountain nodded
or maybe the monkey only needed the
mountain to nod. At any rate the
monkey returned to his own kind a
gentler sort, having given up some-
thing that was difficult to give up
and having communed with the
mountain, with fervor and humility, here
in the new time of monkeys and mountains.

First You Walk

The path is damp.
Dew most likely.
The holiday houses
are bright
like a gallery.
The morning is opening.
I am outside, moving.
This is not what
I meant to say.
I meant to tell you about
the path.
The path is damned.

Someone Told Me It's All Happening at the Zoo

The bonobos came out to
greet us. We hadn't
visited in a while.
They told us the capybaras
were expecting,
the liger started drinking
again, and
the creeping voles,
well, no one knows what's
going on with the creeping voles.
They haven't been the same
since the canis lupus
moved in next door.
We thanked them for the
latest, began our
peregrinations with the falcon.
All the birds were praying.
Later, in front
of the larger cats, we were
feeling uneasy.
Something about the way they
wore their hats,
something about the redecoration
they had done
with the bones of latecomers.
That evening,
at home we ran down
all that we had seen, thankful
again to be the top
of the food chain,
and to understand the need for
our cages, which lock on the inside.

Jack and the Tower of Babel

The loss of the family cow
wasn't really the crux
of the problem. My mother
thought me a simp.
But, friends, it wasn't a hand-
ful of beans I wanted.
It was a ladder, a ladder to Heaven.

Bookseller

There is a book which
once opened you can never
release.
There is the book which
tells you the secret things
you'd rather not know.
There is the book which
teaches love
but its cost is harmful to
various parts of the body.
There is the book, or series
of books, which
tempt children from their homes
to lead them into
the woods, to live
lives feral and dangerous, to
lead lives they wish to lead.
There is the book about books,
an orbicular invention,
an iterative invention, iterative.
There is a book where
words don't get in the way,
a book which damns you.
And there is the final book.
I can show it to you,
but then I must leave you alone
with it which makes
many customers uncomfortable.
This I understand. It's my job.

Sortilege

Out under big
round hoops of moonlight

a crow's shadow
eclipses two lovers,

their kiss tasting dark
suddenly. And ever since

a slight discomfort between
them, a suspicion.

Hoagy Carmichael's Cigarette

Is a numinous object,
removed by time and élan
from its murderous reputation.
It dangles like a modifier,
keeps beat, nods its hothead to
every ropedancer on the floor.
Hoagy Carmichael's cigarette
wants to take you home,
staying till the eggs run out,
underneath buttermilk skies, in
the land of the unfortunate colored man.

It Was a Test Was What They Told Us

We all sat around in the room-sized room.
It was a test. That's what they told us.
Perhaps the sitting was part of it.
And perhaps we were waiting for it to begin.
The guy to the right of me had only one eye.
I told him I wish I didn't have two.
The woman who shut us in was as lovely as dawn.
She had those breasts that make men swine.
After about an hour Jeff said maybe we should do something.
We asked Jeff to sit down and shut up.
After twenty-four hours a few of us were hungry.
After a week there was not much to say.
A year or so later the ones who remained were still smiling.
I didn't really want to belong. I said that for a while.
Then I stopped talking. Just in case the test, you know, had started.

Remember My Name

Let me be obtrusive. The past is
never past. I want to be like
a surgery. You cannot dowse me
like a guttering flame.
In your dreams, there I am, a smile
like a slit in an apple's perfect skin.

Poem Written at Night in September of 2001

And these nights are filled with the insane feeling that something is about to happen that has never happened before, indeed that the impoverished reason of day cannot even conceive of.
—Robert Musil

A poem written with bone,
a dead poem.
A night without stars.

Awake at all hours I rattle
about in the yard.
The moon is a castoff rind.

I return to do the only thing
that seems to make
sense, write. The poem dies.

The Thomas Pynchon Tower

"[H]e found in entropy or the measure of disorganization for a closed system an adequate metaphor to apply to a certain phenomena in his own world."

You can stand next to it.
Its shade is not comfortable.
Its stories, too many to count,
a nonfixable number,
are stacked one on another.
Except when they're not.
You can enter at any time.
You can go to any floor.
But, listen: if you are timid and
you think the past is more
fixed than the future
The Thomas Pynchon Tower
may not be the place for you.
And the face, up there in
one of the opaque windows,
that's the face of Dali's watch.
There are few places as exciting
as the TPT. Ask anyone.
The man there talking into his
lapel. He knows some of the
answers and none of the questions.
Yet he is a familiar in the Tower.
He's as familiar as the talking
dog, as the Christ Child
and his warm-up band. Now, you
feel like one of the denizens.
Now, you feel welcome.
This is as good as it gets here at
The Thomas Pynchon Tower.

Nocturne

At the edge of our yard
we scrutinize the sky,
graying. A light mist
peppers us as if the moon
were spitting. We turn
our faces upward, night blooms.

My Aunt Agni

My Aunt Agni
sends me a personal note.
Stop dreaming,
you little jerk, and do some
real work.
My Aunt Agni
only wants what's best for
me, I think.
She's my mother's ugly
sister but we all
love her for her songs and
the way she does
the laundry.
Dear Aunt Agni, I write back,
There's a platypus
on the playground. There's
a gyroscope
in the master bedroom.
This makes Aunt Agni
stop writing me altogether.
I miss her now. I
wish I had been more
practical. I
think about getting a job,
one my Aunt Agni will
be proud of. Maybe then
she will let me
write her again, with my
atonal music
and my love for the stranger
manifestations of
Eden's First Nomenclature.
Dear Aunt Agni,
I will start. Dear deaf
dead Aunt Agni,
I will start my best letter
to her, my Aunt Agni.

Backspace

for Laurie

The man I was.
Your apartment
where we
couldn't go.
The fearsome
telephone.
The friends who
saw us together.
How funny
you were, how
funny.
Our fitting,
piece to piece.
The morning I
woke, riding
me, that position.
The goodbye
that was not goodbye.
The disappearance.
The sudden
extinction.
The wrenching,
twisting tunnel.
How love does
not affix,
how it's not love.
The man I was.

An Afternoon at the Ono Lennons

John Lennon and I
sat down in the white room.
He asked if I wanted
to play the piano. The piano
was as forbidding as
the gates of Eden. I demurred.
I told John I had read
his books. This pleased him
beyond the mania
that surrounded his other art.
Late in the day
Yoko made some tea. The
three of us just sat there
watching the sun paint
waterliles on the walls.
Finally, I had to leave and
my parting was bittersweet.
John embraced me
at the door. Yoko looked at
me with her widow eyes,
so full of love,
and wisdom, and a third thing.
It was that third thing
I took home with me, which
sits in me still,
like a heart as heavy as the
host, as heavy as that piano,
so white you'd swear you'd died.

Cloudmountaincalling

The white mountain in the distance
is only cloud.
The voice in the receiver is youth.
The heat you feel when you enter the
other room is other people.
The phone is one more hang up. The
moisture on your cheek,
which you thought was desire, is only
the mountain.

There's a Long Line at the New Poem

There's a long line at the New Poem.
The guy with the monkey
is flirting with the girl whose tattoo
changes with the light.
The crowd has waited days. Some slept
on the carpeted freeway leading here.
Others arrived with their mother's fever
in a lunchbox, wrapped in
cellophane. The rumors have it that the
New Poem will open any day
now. The line is patient. The line is just
about the best thing about the
New Poem, but don't tell that to the girl
with the monkey tattoo, or
the guy whose gender changes with the
light. It's a secret that
the New Poem will never really open. It's
an open secret. The final
test will be how long the line lasts, the
line waiting outside the New Poem,
the one that almost stops here….

The Instructions: How to Get There

I'll sit at my desk all day
if it takes that to reach abstraction.

I drink my coffee left-handed
so it feels like a caress.

I look at pictures of people I hold dear.
Their faces are approximations.

The sunlight hitting the page is
the color of a cat, one I remember vaguely.

The first word I have today is
one I have kept in abeyance. The last word, too.

The dog turns around three times and
settles near my memory of the cat.

I will sit at my desk all day
if it takes that to reach obstruction.

What I meant to say was instruction.
The instructions say, go on. They say, go on.

The Box

Every day I put the box out in the sun.
I expected the gods to place there
the final instructions.
Every morning I visit the box and
every morning I am disappointed.
The box remains empty and my life a
a torturous track to nowhere.
I see now that there are more boxes
in the sun. I see now that almost
everyone has placed a box in the sun, a
line now as long as death's logic.
This does not diminish the necessity of
my own box. It shines like a star!

It Was That Kind of Hero, Sweetheart

I feel you slipping away ...
—John Lennon

I sat on the porch smoking my
last John Lennon.
The kids in the neighborhood
were playing with their
weapons in the sprinkler. They
knew things I wanted to
know. As the light changed
into something less formal
I reached for my
glass of Kurt Vonnegut. I
wanted to drain it to the dregs
but temperance ruled
the moment. It was the last of
him, also. My wife came out later.
She stood, legs akimbo,
and let the children see her famous
shadows. She turned to
me with a healthy breast and said,
Do you want Leonard Cohen
for dinner? I had to
scream after her as she left the sunshine:
He's still alive!
It's a dangerous neighborhood, I told
the wife over dinner that night.
She said, it's only as bad as the most
recent sainthood. I chewed
on that, meditatively, as they say.
I chewed and chewed
because it was one tough poet,
a poet whose name escapes me for now.

Phoenix

They've piled
fresh lumber

in the yard

of the burned-out
duplex.

Our First Voyage to Ataraxia

As Romantics we long for that oceanic feeling we felt in the womb, when we were divine and fed by ambrosia.
—Robert Bly

Our knapsacks full of vitamins
we set out for Ataraxia.
The first mate said there would
be sights to see so
we opened our eyes.
The waters rose like a watered rose.
The sky was the color
of a jungle pig.
The first mate said that he once had
a sister who seized.
This was scant comfort.
The morning after the first night we
woke up like rats on a grain ship.
We were biddable.
Our heads were full of isolation.
The sun was the color of the sun
we had dreamed of.
The doctor took the temperature
and ran with it.
We were all family, that was the
paramount truth. And when Ataraxia
finally came in sight
we decided as one that we would
sail around a little longer.

We used our knapsacks
the way Gorgons use their peepers.
Someone mentioned the Golden
Fleece. Someone mentioned
Charybdis. All I know is that if I
ever get back home I am
going to call everyone I used to know
and tell them the best
advertisements in my heart. I will tell
them that I have returned
from Ataraxia, though, in truth, we
never went back there.
In truth we all thought we knew, ultimately, what was best.

The Committee in My Head

The committee in my head
keeps minutes that last for hours.
At all hours I wake to hear
the committee tell me things I'd
rather not hear. Last night
they told me again that I am dying.
That pain in your chest, they
said, it's the devil's drummer.
I listen to the committee because
it's better than talking to myself.
The committee tells me this, too.

How the Hero One Day Sat

On this side of the page
the hero waits like a dog under a tree.
He knows something horrible
is just around the corner.
It must be so if he is to continue to be
the hero. Yet the shade
draws him as sweetly as pure evil.
Inside the tree he can hear the mechanics
of life, the click and buzz of the
élan vital. The hero sits. He sits for
the first time in his heroic life, or at least
that's how he feels. He thinks, I
can just sit here. I can
be as still as the tree, as still as its
shadow. And it was then that
he gave up on being a hero.
It was then that he became a poet.
Now, on this side of the page he
writes his first words of poetry. He
still feels like a dog under a tree
but now his eyes widen, his
heart opens and he, rightly or wrongly,
lets his head yawn into song.

The Man With the Perfect Jump Shot

How he leaves the ground
from the balls of his feet;
how his hands carve a slow
unfolding as the ball leaves
them; how his eye follows
the arc through the cotton
net (what we call string
music) even back to earth.
The man with the perfect jump shot
is playing his game.
Everybody picks him first;
he is constantly surrounded.
He is like the groom at
the reception. He is like
the poet only in heaven.
His is a grace born like Mozart
was born and a rhythm timed
to the planet's rotation
which is not unlike the
spin of the basketball on its
absolute flight. The crowd
holds its collective breath when
he releases. The air fairly
hums with expectancy. But there
is no tension present: the man

with the perfect jump shot
never misses. Rainbow after rainbow
as natural as light. A divine
trajectory. And tonight the man
with the perfect jump shot is
in our gymnasium; he is on our
team. Tomorrow he may be elsewhere.
Tomorrow he may be against us.
But tonight, here in our tiny
world, tonight, thanks be to God
in his wisdom, we are playing
with the man with the perfect jump
shot. We say it to ourselves
to be reassured: the man with the
perfect jump shot is on our team.
The man with the perfect jump shot
loves us. He would do anything for
us, even die. The man. The man
with the perfect jump shot.

God

I dressed in the robes.
I was your acolyte.
In my middle years I lost you,
the way one puts
something in a pocket and for-
gets about it.
Now I see you there in the glint
off the ice, in the unfurling
of my daughter's wings.
I see you in the keyboard, in
the verso, in the game
we play with our knowing.

Recent Developments in Home Schooling

Most of our problems proceed from our inability to sit quietly in a small room.

—Pascal

They nailed the door shut.
I opened my mouth
and a string of similes fell out.
The day broke outside
like a tractor erupting.
My wife waved from
the driveway, the children around
her like a ring of toadstools.
I started a book. What else could
I do? The first line was
To Reader with approbation.
It put me down so I put it down.
And another thing: you
must stop calling me, calling me home.

Closer to Home

The backyard is bathed
in soapy moonlight.
The bean trees gather their
bugs and rattle like
maracas. In the time it takes
for me to step outside
the dog stops its singing.
I whisper from the stoop
the night's secret name.

KKK

One of my first memories of Memphis.
I was five, newly arrived.
At the downtown Christmas parade
they were there handing out leaflets
for an upcoming rally. My father
crumpled his into an angry ball and
threw it away as if spitting. They
haunted me like dream figures, like
any secret association. I later
saw them in robes at the Mid-South
Fair, marching like nuns, looking for
yokels, part of the ongoing freak show.

The Judge's Narcolepsy

Everybody knows the war is over. Everybody knows the good guys lost.
—Leonard Cohen

How we used the words we were
told to use. How
we suffered under the withering
gazes. How the room
filled with a perfume from the
abattoir. We stood
up when they said to stand up.
We left the decision making to all
the others. We died,
sentence by sentence. How we feel
about that. How we sleep.

Lizard

A lizard the color of the light
off a saucepan
skitters out from under the trash
can. A brief sighting
like a flash in the dark. I am
temporarily joyous
and then the earth swallows it,
the way a shadow swallows a spark.

Watching Things Fall From a Distance

It was Bobby's 22.
We shot at birds mostly.
Later we found a
pig rotting in a ditch.
Bobby shot a cat also.
We were carefree,
young, full of ourselves.
Later we grew up and
discovered divorce
and depression.
Death we already knew,
though our first lessons
were primitive.
Losing brother and parent
was something else.
What I remember most is
that it was cold and our
breath hung in the air
like mercy. We pulled that
trigger over and over.
Watching things fall
from a distance.

Corinthian

I used to love the Beatles.
Now they are just so much noise,
so much background screech.
I used to love art, big
messy art, with things in it.
Now, I say art doesn't need
anyone. It is cold like a drill.
I used to love the TV.
It showed me things at a young
age, things I haven't forgotten.
It was hard to stop loving
the TV. It had been so constant.
And I used to love my friends,
now gone hoary and hairy
and full of old wind. I used
to love them fervently because
I didn't want to ever be alone.
I used to love you, Sweetheart.
Put down the bazooka. Take
my hand. I am about to tell
you how that changed, too.
I am about to eschew the last
thing I will ever love, my sweetheart.

Knitting

Under the lamp
my wife sits knitting.
Her hands form a small cap
to be given to our
daughter's friend.
Her face is lovely in repose.
Her concentration
is starlight.
The cap unfolds like a tiny
life, one I almost missed.

Execution

I hear your name
in the cock's crow.
I pierce the sun
with the sword you used
when I was crucified.
The scar on my side
is the shape of your smile.

Voice

Death is constant. We
know this. But worse
is the voice that never
stops, never stops.
It is ice breaking inside
us, calving and carving
us with its honed blade.
It tells us things we do
not want to know. It
tells us things after the
things we did not want
to know. It keeps sleep
at bay. Even in sleep
it comes as waves, the
dreams of a story that will
swallow us. We will wake
and the voice will be
there again, as alive as our
desire to stop, to rest.
The voice will tell us it is
our best friend. It will
tell us the story of ourselves,
the version where we get
to live, beyond even death,
beyond, beyond the silence.

Too Much Talk

You said, there. Touch
it. I said,
Maybe we ought to start
at the begging.
You said, lemme take
a bit of
your cloud. I said, honey,
I want your honey.
You said, I said, no too
many times. I said,
but you said nothing
mattered except
the way our fingers snapped.
I said, that
was the monkey I was
traveling on.
You said, I said too much.
I said, but
maybe, in the end, that's
what it will take.
It will take us both saying
everything.
You said, don't be a ninny.
I'm hanging you,
now. I said, that's ok. I
only really
called to talk about
ending things.
Like sentences, sentences
of death.

Passing a Playground at Night

Moonlight
on a silver slide.
It's too late

for children to be out.

Habitant

The years go by. The women
I loved will not talk to me.
I take my heart out to the marshes
and study the rising and falling
of birds. More years go by.
The time I have spent thinking about
the past weighs on me like
Marley's chains. I take my heart out
to the marketplace and study
the rushing and bumping of the many.
All the women I have loved, I say
to the telephone. I say to the
windows and the door. I take my
heart out and dissect it with a
semi-colon and a comma. All I know
about the past is that it rises
and falls like birds. I have learned
little. I study the inconsistent beating
of my heart, sore now from privity.

Chloe at Dusk

Even before it's quite dark enough
Chloe comes to me with wide eyes
and anticipation. It's time to
catch lightning bugs, she tells me,
as if for the first time.
Together we go out into the gloaming,
the sky the tint of a frying pan,
the front porch an oasis of
between-world calm. Chloe hurries
down the steps and looks about her,
spinning madly. They're all
around us, she says, and I imagine
she is right. But, for now,
from this vantage point, higher up and
further away, I see nothing.
Only the putty colored air
and Chloe, her dress a whirly, dancing.

Graceland

I went to scoff and, chastened,
stayed to pray. I prayed
that there would be something
at the end for all of us,
something more than a cold
bathroom floor. Someone
handed me a candle, already lit.
Someone handed me a poem.

A Penultimate Parley

Quick, before the light fades.
What did it feel like?
It felt like the beginning of death but not death.
What led you here?
The same fragile things which led you.
What is your name, now?
It is as it was. I am called before you with
no name.
What will it be like, after the darkness comes?
It will be the beginning of the
end but not the end. Stop. Let me ask you
the final questions.
What is there now that wasn't? What is there
about us that is different?
What does my next breath signify if not that
you are near, that you are all I love
and hold dear?
What next?
This we never ask. This is a question
made of silence.

Before the Great Troubling

There were times of great clarity.
There were days when time
did not imprison, did not
glad-hand the devil.
And there was a feeling that this
would all go on, getting
better and better,
enriching us in ways we could never
foresee. This was the feeling
we lived under as if
it were shade.
There were times, before the great
troubling, when we
were happy to think the world vast
and shapeless, when
we were happy to call modernity
our host. This I remind myself
when it closes in.
This comforts somehow
as if in the past is the seed of a
future where I will
once again walk out into the dark-
ness as if it were my
best dream, as if it held things for me
that I would need, things
as particular and personal as a poem.

COREY MESLER has published in numerous journals and anthologies. He has published four novels, *Talk: A Novel in Dialogue* (2002), *We Are Billion-Year-Old Carbon* (2006), *The Ballad of the Two Tom Mores* (2010) and *Following Richard Brautigan* (2010), and a book of short stories, *Listen* (2008).

His first full-length poetry collection, *Some Identity Problems* (2008), is out from Foothills Publishing. He has been nominated for the Pushcart Prize numerous times, and two of his poems were chosen for Garrison Keillor's *Writer's Almanac*. He has two children, Toby and Chloe. With his wife, he runs Burke's Book Store, one of the country's oldest (1875) and best independent bookstores. He also claims to have written "These Boots are Made for Walking." He can be found at www.coreymesler.com.

List of Publication Credits

American Poetry Journal: "Memoir"
Barn Owl Review: "It was a Test, Was What they Told Us"
Big Tex(t): "Removing Stumps"
Blackmail Press: "The Judge's Narcolepsy"
Blood Orange: "The First Lovefall"
Boxcar Poetry: "Those Melville Silences"
Brink Magazine: "Someone Told me It's All Happening at the Zoo"
Cause and Effect: "My Novel Life"
Chantarelle's Notebook: "Chloe at 3"
Contemporary American Voices: "The Box" and "How the Hero One Day Sat"
Cotyledon: "Passing a Playground at Night"
Counterexample Poetics: "Ash"
Dark Sky: "Sandra, I am Almost Finished" and "My Aunt Agni"
Dead Mule: "Elvis in Elvisland"
Deep Cleveland Oracle: "Execution"
Dogmatika: "There's a Long Line at the New Poem" and "Before the Great Troubling"
Driftwood Review: "Lizard"
Farmhouse: "Closer to Home"
Flutter: "God"
Fou: "The Monkey and the Mountain"
Free Verse: "Sortilege"
Goblin Fruit: "The Fairy Tale Wife"
Goldwake Press: "Graceland"
High Horse: "Nightstand Poem"
Horse Less Review: "Phoenix"

Houston Literary Review: "The Poem of the World" "Jack and the Tower of Babel" "In the Salinger Building There are Nine Stories" and "Pray"
Inscribed: "My Father's Death is a Small Box"
Journal of Truth and Consequences: "First There is a Mountain, Then there is no Mountain, Then There Is"
Ken*Again: "Nature Jar"
Kill Author: "Out Again" and "13 Ways of Looking at a Blackboard"
Kill Poet: "First You Walk"
Lamplighter Review: "Voice"
Lily: "Educationalist"
Lucid Rhythms: "The Comma"
Mississippi Crow: "It was that Kind of Hero, Sweetheart" and "Corinthian"
Mitochondria: "Hell, the Whole Kingdom Sucks"
Monongahela Review: "See Me"
My Favorite Bullet: "Joe Zen"
Nuvein: "The Infection of City"
Otoliths: "Nocturne"
Past Simple: "The Barbarian Heart" "A Treasure Hid in a Field" and "Life During Wartime"
Pegasus Review: "Bookseller"
Pen and Ink: "Knitting"
Poetic Diversity: "Regret"
Poetry Super Highway: "Tell Me if You Think This is Going to be a Problem"
Quill and Ink: "See Me"
Raven Poetry: "In my Dream Emily Mortimer"
Ray Succre's *The Rat*: "Habitant"
Razor Wire: "Poem Written at Night in September 2001"

Right Hand Pointing: "Opening" "My John Lennon Period" and "Opening 2"
Rumble: "Our History of the Book"
Sawbuck: "The Halloween Between Us"
Shampoo: "Watching Things Fall from a Distance"
Smartish Pace: "Memoir"
Softblow: "Backspace" "Recent Developments in Home Schooling" and "The Instructions: How to Get There"
Southern Gothic: "Elvis in Elvisland"
Spare Change: "Remember my Name"
Stone Table Review: "An Afternoon at the Ono Lennons"
The Legendary: "Simply Again Simply"
Tipton Poetry Journal: "My Thomas Pynchon"
Tonic: "Colloquy in the Void"
trnsfr: "My Dog Talks to Me"
Umbrella: "The Thomas Pynchon Tower"
Underground Window: "Those Hitchcock Silences"
Visions International: "The Man with the Perfect Jump Shot"
Vulcan: "The Sleeping Saviors"
Wandering Army: "Our First Voyage to Ataraxia"
Whalelane: "After Reading The Tao of the Jump Shot"
Wilderness House Literary Review: "We Were Told to Wait Here" and "The Observer Observed"
Word Riot: "Bell's Palsy 1" "Cloudmountaincalling" and "An Email Poem"
Words Words Words: "We Are All Connected"
WTF: "Hoagy Carmichael's Cigarette" and "The Committee in my Head"
Xconnect: "Chloe at Dusk"
Ygdrasil : "Sleepe, Angry Beauty"

In addition these poems appeared in these publications:

"The Poem of the World" "The Barbarian Heart" "The Halloween Between Us" "Hell, the Whole Kingdom Sucks" "Jack and the Tower of Babel" "Phoenix" in the chapbook, *Grit* (Amsterdam Press, 2008)

"Elvis in Elvisland" in the chapbook, *Dark on Purpose* (Little Poem Press, 2004)

"Nature Jar" "Chloe at Dusk" "Chloe at 3" in the chapbook, *The Chloe Poems* (Maverick Duck Press, 2007)

"Those Hitchcock Silences" "Those Melville Silences" in the chapbook, *Pictures from Lang and Fellini* (Sheltering Pines Press, 2007)

"Passing a Playground at Night" in the chapbook, *Chin-Chin in Eden* (Still Waters Press, 2003)

"The Man with the Perfect Jump Shot" in the anthology, *Full Court* (Breakaway Books, 1996)

"Knitting" in the anthology, *Knit Lit the Third* (Three Rivers Press, 2005)

"Sleepe, Angry Beauty" in the chapbook, *The Hole in Sleep* (Wood Works, 2006)

www.ingramcontent.com/pod-product-compliance
Lightning Source LLC
Chambersburg PA
CBHW071731090426
42738CB00011B/2453